Nation's
Restaurant News

RESTAURANT MANAGER'S POCKET HANDBOOK

MENU DESIGN

25 KEYS TO

Profitable
Success

DAVID V. PAVESIC, F.M.P.

Copyright© 1999 by David V. Pavesic, Ph.D.
Lebhar-Friedman Books

Lebhar-Friedman Books is a company of Lebhar-Friedman Inc.

Printed in the United States of America

Library of Congress Cataloging-in-Publication Data

Pavesic, David V.
    Restaurant manager's pocket handbook : 25 keys to
profitable success. Menu design / David V. Pavesic.
      p. cm.
    Includes index.
    ISBN 0-86730-754-4 (pbk.)
    1. Menus 2. Food service--Marketing. I. Title.
TX911.3.M45P38 1998
642--dc21   98-39303
                                               CIP

THE STARTING POINT for every new restaurant concept is the menu. When a family member, friend, or colleague suggests that you try a restaurant, one of the first questions you ask is, "What kind of food do they serve?" That draws attention immediately to the menu. A restaurant's menu is far more than a printed bill of fare. It's a critical element in communicating to the customer not only what is served but also the personality and character of the restaurant.

The menu is the one piece of printed advertising that an operator virtually is assured the customer will read. External advertising and promotion draws customers into the restaurant, and that's where the menu takes over. Its design can influence what a customer will order and how much he or she will spend. The design also can be used to direct a customer's attention and feature certain items. Historical records of the menu-sales mix allow you to increase the accuracy of your forecasts for purchasing, preparation, and scheduling.

Given the importance of the menu, it's surprising how little time and attention are given to its design and printing. After reading this book, you will have a new respect for the menu and the role it plays in the profitability of your restaurant.

25 KEYS TO
MENU DESIGN

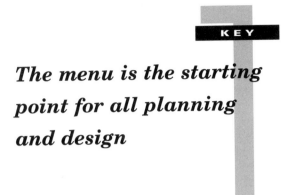

The menu is the starting point for all planning and design

PLANNING FOR ANY RESTAURANT concept begins with the menu. A well-designed menu will help you determine such key elements of your operation as the size of the kitchen, the equipment you require, skill levels of your preparation and service staffs, and design and decor of the interior and exterior of the building. And since the menu is the foundation of the business, it must be given serious thought and consideration before you commit yourself financially to a particular location.

If you have a specific menu and restaurant concept in mind, be careful when selecting a location. Conversely, if you have a specific location in mind, you must take care when selecting a concept. Location remains critically important to the success of a restaurant. If you have the wrong menu and concept for a particular loca-

> **"Don't delay acting on a good idea. Chances are someone else has just thought of it too. Success comes to the one who acts first."**
>
> — ANONYMOUS

tion, the operation may fail.

Your menu choices must appeal to the clientele you expect to serve. If the menu is created without regard for those customers, it is just as big a mistake as selecting the wrong location. While today's consumers certainly are more sophisticated and willing to try new food items than in the past, you must temper your menu with the standard steaks, fish, pasta, and chicken dishes that are found on most menus. The way you prepare and serve those popular items should provide sufficient room for culinary creativity.

Get input from as many individuals as you can. Speak to people who will give you an honest response, not someone who will tell you what they think you want to hear. In fact, if everyone tells you that you have a great idea, it probably means that someone has done it already. On the other hand, if your idea is received with skepticism and uncertainty, you're probably proposing something unique and different.

Many creative ideas sound really good. However, they may not be financially feasible. Conduct a feasibility study with pro-forma income statements and ask others with experience in the business to review the figures you've forecasted. Remember: It's better to be conservative with your sales forecasts and liberal with your expense projections than the other way around. You must use real numbers, not rules of thumb or industry averages.

Of course, you can never expect to remove all of the risk. Sometimes education and experience make us conservative and cautious, so it's good to have some young and naive thinkers on the planning team. At the same time, if you're told that you have a crazy idea and that it's risky, but you feel strongly that it could work, go for it. Most new ideas and concepts are introduced by independent operators and not by the board of directors of the large restaurant chains.

(1) The decor of a restaurant is determined in part by the menu, pricing, and service.

    A. True
    B. False

(2) The equipment selection and layout should be set "before" the menu is written.

    A. True
    B. False

(3) If you have the wrong menu and concept for a particular location, the operation may not succeed even with quality food and service.

    A. True
    B. False

(4) When planning a menu, you should strive to write one that appeals to all types of customers.

    A. True
    B. False

(5) The manager and the chef are the only individuals who should have input into the content of the menu.

    A. True
    B. False

ANSWERS: 1: A, 2: B, 3: A, 4: B, 5: B

The menu is more than just a list of items your kitchen prepares

THE DICTIONARY DEFINES a menu as "a bill of fare" or "a list of food items a restaurant prepares and serves." If that were the case, menus would be no more than printed lists of food and beverage items. The role of a menu must be broad and comprehensive.

The goals of an effective menu can be summarized in five statements. A well-designed menu:

(1) Serves as an effective communication, marketing, and cost-control tool.

(2) Emphasizes what the customer wants and what the restaurant prepares and serves best.

(3) Obtains the check average required to realize sales goals and bottom-line return.

(4) Utilizes staff and equipment in an efficient manner.

(5) Leads to more accurate forecasting of the menu sales mix.

A well-designed menu requires considerable planning and research before it can be finalized. Too much depends on the menu for you not to give it the kind of attention and budget you would allocate to any significant major capital investment. Furthermore, too much depends on the menu for you to delegate its entire development to a chef or manager. Menu design involves a team decision that should include the owner, chef or kitchen manager, dining-room manager, and even customer representatives.

The importance of the menu content and design cannot be overstated. Much of a restaurant's success will be determined by its menu, and the menu-planning and design process must be approached with seriousness and diligence. The menu must be planned from the perspective of the clientele the restaurant hopes to attract, and traditional favorites and adventuresome selections should be included. However, the other aspect of the menu plan should address the operational aspects of food cost, gross profit, average check, purchasing, preparation, and kitchen efficiency.

With those aspects clearly defined, the design of the menu should accentuate the positive goals of the menu plan. Whether you print your own menus in-house, contract the services of a menu-design consultant, or work with a local printer, the operational aspects must be reflected in your menu design. But remember: Nobody can design a menu to accomplish those goals unless you communicate your expectations to them first.

The menu communicates your restaurant's personality to the public

HOW IMPORTANT IS THE MENU in projecting the image or personality of a restaurant? Depending on the type of operation, the menu can be the communication link between the restaurant and the customer. It's especially important to the moderately priced table-service operation whose management or chef are not known to the patrons. The old saying that "you can't judge a book by its cover" shouldn't apply to menus and menu covers. The menu should project an accurate image of what to expect in terms of decor, service formality, price range, and even the type of food served. If a menu design is nondescript or leaves one with an inaccurate perception of the restaurant, it is not communicating with the public.

Imagine that you're planning to visit a new restaurant for the first time. You haven't even

> **"Too many people are thinking of security instead of opportunity. They seem more afraid of life than death."**
>
> — JAMES F. BYRNES

---

seen the restaurant from the outside; you've only heard about it from friends and radio ads. However, a copy of its menu is handed to you. After you put it down, you probably will have developed some expectations about the place, which now must be met, or you will be disappointed.

When you look at the size, color, and graphics employed in the menu, it begins to "communicate" to you. You will begin to develop images in your mind that will in turn influence your expectations about the level of service and whether it's casual or formal, expensive or moderately priced, whether table cloths or place mats will be used — even how you expect the servers to be dressed. A good menu can even convey a sense of the interior decor and color schemes.

Once you have stepped inside, you will be able to compare your perceptions with the actual theme and decor. A well-designed menu should give you a fairly accurate picture of the food, service, and decor; a poorly designed menu will communicate inaccurately. And if expectations aren't met, you may leave dissatisfied.

Traditionally, the owner-operator often emerged as the "personality" of an independent restaurant. The owner — or perhaps even the chef or maître d' — would personally greet and seat customers, distribute menus, and even prepare the food for special customers. The menu was secondary in projecting the restaurant's personality. But today, with 80 percent of restaurant sales being transacted in owner-absentee operations and chains, that type of personal attention can be found in only a few operations.

If a restaurant's personality is dependent upon the personality of the owner, chef, or maître d', consider how that will limit the growth and development of a business. If that person leaves, the business could suffer significantly. Consider too that if the personality of a manager or chef were critical to the success of a restaurant, multiple-unit chains wouldn't exist. While it is a definite bonus to have a "personality" in the restaurant, it is not imperative for success.

Chains have replaced the personality of the owner, chef, or manager with the concept and theme of the restaurant. That is not to say that a good manager doesn't contribute to an operation's image. In fact, I have a saying: "As management goes, so goes the restaurant." The manager remains the key element in an efficiently run, service-minded restaurant. But managers, chefs, and maîtres d' will come and go, while the menu — and the image it communicates — remains the permanent link between the operation and the dining public.

(1) An effectively designed menu can be a valuable marketing, communication, and cost-control tool for management.

    A. True
    B. False

(2) The menu's appearance and design should project an accurate image of a restaurant's decor, service, prices, and type of food served.

    A. True
    B. False

(3) Chains have diminished the importance of the personality of a manager, chef, or maître d', and replaced them with the concept and theme of the restaurant.

    A. True
    B. False

(4) The menu has always been the number one element in projecting the image and personality of a restaurant, even those independently owned and operated.

    A. True
    B. False

(5) The process of menu planning and design must be given the same time and effort as any major financial decision.

    A. True
    B. False

ANSWERS: 1: A, 2: A, 3: A, 4: B, 5: A

The menu is your most important internal marketing tool

THE MENU MAY BE the most important internal advertising device used to sell the customer once he or she is inside your restaurant. It is the only piece of printed advertising that you are virtually 100-percent certain will be read. Once it has been placed in the guest's hand, the menu can influence not only what will be ordered but also how much will be spent. Using forecasted cover counts and average check targets, the menu design directly influences sales revenue. Management constantly forecasts business volume and relates that knowledge to decisions concerning how much to buy, inventory, and prepare. The menu has an impact on each of those decisions.

Increasingly, restaurant companies have come to understand the impact of proper menu design on check averages. Several years ago

Houlihan's revamped its menu with the specific goal of increasing its check averages. The menu was designed to lead the customer from specialty drinks on the cover to appetizers on the first page to complete dinners inside. The chain's old menu, by contrast, lumped all types of items next to one another on the same large fold-out page. Management determined that design might have deflected dinner sales by making it easier for customers to select only an appetizer.

New menu designs are borrowing techniques from the retailing industry that make items stand out and say, "Buy me." An article in the Wall Street Journal described menu designs that highlight the most profitable offerings — items that are also touted by the servers.

The Gallup Organization reported in a study that a customer will spend an average of 109 seconds in reading the menu. Consequently, the time limit must be addressed in your menu design and presentation. T.G.I. Friday's previously offered a menu with over 12 pages; that since has been reduced to six.

A properly designed menu can direct the attention of the diner to specific items and increase the likelihood that those items will be ordered. Those items should be the ones with the highest gross profit and lowest food costs and help achieve the average check needed to return the desired sales. The customer's decision cannot be controlled completely; however, it can be directed and not left entirely to chance.

The menu is a valuable cost-control tool

YOU CAN IMPROVE THE CHANCES of achieving your target food-cost percentage, gross profit, average check, and total sales goals if you design your menu to help you accomplish those goals. If your goal is to hit a 34-percent cost of food sold, you must sell the right mix of menu items to make that average at the end of the month.

Your menu design and pricing strategy can help contain your food cost by forecasting the items that will sell — which in turn will allow you to purchase and prepare optimum amounts. It even can help you to schedule kitchen labor more efficiently because you will know exactly what preparation must be done. And once the daily kitchen routine has been organized, you will be better prepared for business volume, which will improve your ability to

"The best way to escape from a problem is to solve it."

— Alan Saporta

---

get the food out more efficiently and therefore improve customer service.

Menu prices cannot be entirely cost-driven decisions, but cost is at least a starting point. Menu items like chicken, pasta, soups, and salads typically are low in food cost. Unfortunately, they also may be some of the lowest-priced items on the menu. On the other hand, steaks, chops, and seafood items are high in food cost and are some of the higher-priced items on the menu. Consequently, the menu sales mix must comprise items with varying food costs and menu prices.

If you're not achieving your check average or overshooting your food-cost objective, one of the reasons could be your menu. Its design could be working counter to your plans if you're selling too many high or low food-cost items. Remember: If you sell more items with high gross profits, your food cost will increase; if you sell more low food-cost items, your average check and overall sales revenue will decline. Therefore, you should try to sell items that are both low in food cost and high in gross profit. And your menu should highlight those items to increase the likelihood of the customer's selecting them.

When food cost is too high, management first looks at what could be happening in the kitchen, examining purchasing prices, preparation waste, overportioning, and other preparation-related causes. Of course, the problem could be in the dining room if checks are missing or if food is being transferred out of the kitchen without being recorded. If all of those areas have been investigated and are under control, the problem might be in the menu sales mix itself. And the only way to change the sales mix is to change the menu design.

(1) The menu is the only piece of printed advertising that you can be 100-percent assured the customer will pick up and read.

    A. True
    B. False

(2) A properly designed menu will do all but one of the following:

    A. Help control food cost
    B. Optimize sales revenue
    C. Control labor cost

(3) The number of pages in a menu has little impact on the effectiveness of the menu as a merchandising and cost-control tool.

    A. True
    B. False

(4) Which menu items should be emphasized on the menu to increase the likelihood that they will be selected?

    A. High food-cost items
    B. High labor-cost items
    C. Items with the lowest gross profit
    D. Items with low food costs, high gross profits, and priced to optimize average check

(5) A properly designed menu can actually control the customers menu selection.

    A. True
    B. False

ANSWERS: 1: A, 2: C, 3: B, 4: D, 5: A

Give your menu design and production the attention and budget you would any major capital-investment decision

THE MENU IS PERHAPS THE MOST critical factor in the overall success of a restaurant. Everything begins with the menu. Consequently, it must be granted the same attention and study that you would give to such decisions as location, construction, lease, financing, and the articles of incorporation. Too often, the menu design is left to the end and not budgeted for adequately.

Recently, an Atlanta operator spent over $5 million to build, equip, and decorate his restaurant. I was given a copy of the opening menu and found it embarrassingly incongruent with the image the preopening publicity was attempting to convey. The menu was printed simply on 65-pound varnished cover stock without any graphics or illustrations. It was analogous to wearing a pair of casual shoes with a formal tuxedo. The owners had spent $5 million on the restaurant and less than $500 on the menu.

That illustrates how the menu did not communicate accurately the personality of the restaurant. I'm not implying that the more you spend on your menu, the more effective it will be as a communication, cost-control, and marketing tool. Some restaurants have menus designed by Bill Blass and Pierre Cardin that are truly works of art and cost thousands of dollars. But while those designer menus might amuse and entertain the customer, they fail miserably at doing what a menu should do. And that is to guide the customer's attention to the items the restaurant prepares best and wants to sell most.

Many of the menus that win prizes at the annual National Restaurant Show are works of art and masterfully printed. They're shaped like artists, palettes, contain custom art work, and are printed in full color. But they're not judged on how effectively they sell the menu items that management would like to sell. In fact, the question "Which items do you want to stand out on the menu?" probably was never discussed with the designer and printer. Supplied with the correct information, your menu designer can use his or her expertise to showcase those items.

When it comes to the cost of producing a menu, printing probably is the least expensive element of the process. The cost will be in the menu-sales mix analysis and the graphic design used to promote the items that will help you lower food cost, increase gross profit, and optimize average check.

Menu-sales analysis reveals the items you need to feature

MENU-SALES ANALYSIS is the process that tracks the popularity of each menu item by recording the number sold. Taking that process together with each item's price and food cost, you're in a position to examine the menu-sales mix in great detail.

One of the purposes of sales analysis is to identify the menu items that must be emphasized on the menu. When profit projections are not realized, an operator's first response often is to adjust menu prices and food costs. But it can be shortsighted to conclude that lost sales revenues and profits are due solely to poor purchases, overportions, rising costs, or excessive waste. The problem may in fact stem from the mix of menu items.

Initially, some operators might focus on food-cost percentage alone and attempt to sell

> **"To change and to change for the better are two different things."**
>
> — GERMAN PROVERB

---

only items with the lowest food-cost percentages. But that strategy has a downside: While the food-cost percentage might be low, the average check and overall sales revenue might remain flat or even decline. The reason? Many of the low food-cost items being offered are the lowest-priced items on the menu, which tends to lower the overall average check. Unless a restaurant serves a greater number of customers each meal period, the overall sales revenue will fall.

Many operators look at the individual gross-profit return of menu items and ignore food cost entirely. Proponents of the gross-profit approach argue, "You bank dollars, not percentages." Those individuals concentrate on selling menu items with high individual gross profit — that is, what remains after food cost has been deducted from the menu price. That approach leads to the promotion of such items as steaks and seafood rather than pasta and chicken. But a direct consequence is an increase in the food-cost percentage because the items with the greatest gross profit also have the highest food-cost percentages.

As long as customer counts remain constant, that approach will work. It tends to be most successful in country clubs, resorts, and commercial markets where price inelasticity is present. However, many operators find that in highly competitive markets, the strategy is not successful. Customer counts fall because prices are perceived as being higher than those of competitors — especially those expounding low food cost as their strategy.

Both of those methods treat low food cost and high individual gross profit as being mutually exclusive. In other words, items with low food costs will have low gross profits, while items with high gross profits will have high food costs. But that's not the case. Consider that the optimum menu-sales mix is one that simultaneously optimizes total dollar gross profit — not individual gross profit — and total sales revenue, while keeping food-cost percentage as low as possible.

(1) A menu can be a "work of art" and not be an effective merchandising and cost-control tool.

    A. True
    B. False

(2) The printer will not need your input on which menu items should be singled out for emphasis in the menu design.

    A. True
    B. False

(3) An effective menu design can be accomplished without menu-sales analysis being conducted.

    A. True
    B. False

(4) Giving only high gross-profit items emphasis on your menu can cause your food cost to increase.

    A. True
    B. False

(5) Low food cost and high gross profit are mutually exclusive attributes. In other words, a single menu item cannot achieve both.

    A. True
    B. False

ANSWERS: 1: A, 2: B, 3: B, 4: A, 5: B

Cost-margin analysis helps pinpoint menu designing, pricing, and packaging decisions

COST-MARGIN ANALYSIS is a methodology used to analyze the menu-sales mix that reduces the inherent biases of both the gross-profit and food-cost approaches previously described. The name reflects both food-cost and contribution-margin (also known as gross-profit) criteria in its analysis. Cost-margin analysis examines each menu item from three perspectives: whether it is popular or unpopular, high or low in food cost, and high or low in contribution margin.

Cost-margin analysis emphasizes that *total or weighted contribution margin* is more relevant than the *individual gross profit* of an item. Building on the statement that "we bank dollars, not percentages," the total gross-profit dollars generated by a popular menu item with a moderate individual gross profit will far exceed the total dollars from an unpopular menu item with a high individual gross profit. Let's examine two menu items. Item "A" sells for $3.65 and returns a $2.22 gross profit; "B" sells for $4.95 and returns a $2.70 gross profit. "A" sold 269 orders, while "B" sold only 115. The total or weighted gross profit from "A" was $597.18, while "B" generated only $310.50. "A" is a popular item with a lower gross profit and lower food-cost percentage than "B"; as a result, it puts more dollars into the register.

Cost-margin classifies each menu item into one of four categories: *Primes, Problems, Standards, and Sleepers*. Primes are popular menu items that have a low food cost and a high contribution margin. Operators want to work hardest to increase the sales of those items. Standards are popular menu items with high food costs and high contribution margins. Those items tend to be the steak and seafood entrées. Sleepers are unpopular menu items with low contribution margins and low food-cost percentages. Problems are those unpopular menu items that are high in food cost and low in contribution margin.

Once items are placed in one of the four categories, various tactics such as improved menu design, new menu pricing, and marketing methodology can be employed to help the overall sales mix.

Maximize cost-margin analysis in menu design and pricing decisions

9

ONCE MENU ITEMS have been classified as being either *Prime, Problem, Standard or Sleeper*, specific strategies can be employed to correct the weaknesses or optimize the strengths of each dish.

Every restaurant needs to have several Primes on its menu. Those popular items tend to be the signature foods or house specialties and are as close to monopoly items as you can get in a restaurant. Consequently, in the short run, take advantage of your monopoly and try increasing the price from 25 cents to 95 cents. If demand doesn't decline, that item has price elasticity. Primes should be given high visibility on the menu and promoted internally through suggestive selling by servers. Monitor quality and presentation to ensure high standards and serve abundant portions.

> **"One's mind, once stretched by a new idea, never regains its original dimensions."**
>
> — OLIVER WENDELL HOLMES

Standards are popular menu items that have higher-than-average food costs but still generate high gross-profit dollars. Every restaurant will have several Standards on the menu, such as prime rib or shrimp. The only downside to selling too many of those items is that your overall food-cost percentage will rise. However, you can take several steps to reduce the negative side effects. First, as with Primes, test for price inelasticity by increasing the price a little. Even if the number sold declines as a result, you will have decreased your food cost while increasing your gross profit on each sale. Or, if you feel a price increase will result in a decline in sales, explore the possibility of reducing portion sizes while holding your current price. If portions cannot be reduced, consider reducing or eliminating one of the accompaniments and price it à la carte. If neither can be done, reduce the negative aspects of selling too many by relocating it to low-profile position on the menu to limit its chance of selection. In its place promote a low-cost item, or Sleeper, to soften the impact of those high-cost items.

Sleepers are unpopular items that have a low food cost and a low contribution margin. The fact that they're slow sellers is perhaps the greatest contributing factor to their having such a low contribution margin. Sleepers are often new menu items being tested in the hopes that they will become Primes. In fact, they must be promoted heavily to increase the likelihood of being ordered by the guest. Reposition Sleepers to increase their visibility on the menu and promote them with suggestive selling techniques, table tents, and menu boards. Because Sleepers have lower-than-average food costs, their prices can be reduced as incentives for purchase. Offering additional accompaniments is yet another way to get customers to try a new item. Or you can try increasing portion sizes. If the Sleeper is a unique item, rename it and market it as a signature of your restaurant.

Lastly, we have the menu items known as Problems. They are not popular, have a high food cost and have a low contribution margin. Before you remove them from the menu, however, you can try several things to improve their food cost and contribution margin. The first thing you might consider is to raise the price to lower the food cost. However, that could further diminish the items' popularity. Next, examine their positioning on the menu — it could be a reason for low sales. If prices cannot be raised, consider reducing portions or accompaniments or else combine with lower-cost ingredients.

Remember: The decision to remove an item from the menu is not based on quantitative reasons alone. Many of the items classified as Problems are children's menu items, which are priced low to encourage parents to bring children to the restaurant. Many children's portions are sold at cost or at a low markup. An item should be removed from the menu only if it is a poor seller, serves no marketing purpose, and requires costly, perishable ingredients that are not used in any other preparation.

The techniques of 'menu psychology' can make things easier for the operator

"MENU PSYCHOLOGY" TECHNIQUES are borrowed from the retailing industry, which employs window, counter, and mannequin displays to boost sales. The menu is to a restaurant what the merchandise display is to a major department store. You want your customers to see all the things you have for sale in the hope that they will find something they like and ultimately make a purchase.

Any menu, design, or format will produce a predictable sales mix if put in service every day for a prolonged period of time. If such a pattern occurs without any rhyme or reason to the design of the menu, think of the possibilities if the menu were specifically designed to promote the items you wanted to sell. Instead of leaving sales entirely to chance, you actually could guide the customers' attention to those items.

A properly designed menu can help any foodservice operation achieve its sales goals, keep costs in line, maintain speed of preparation and service, and return a desired profit. But that doesn't happen by accident: It must be planned. There are certain practices that, when incorporated into the graphic design and layout of a menu, can influence a guest's selection.

Such practices and techniques aren't subliminal, nor do they force or trick the customer into ordering something that's not wanted. But much like a television commercial or newspaper advertisement, menu design can put an idea into the head of the consumer and thereby increase the likelihood that he or she at least will consider purchasing a particular item.

The well-designed menu can help management sell certain items more often than if the items were randomly placed on the menu. Certainly, these techniques cannot make an unpopular item popular or make liver and onions outsell southern fried chicken. But they can help sell more orders of liver and onions than if the item were randomly placed on the menu.

Specific design techniques can increase the likelihood of a customer's selecting a particular item

"MENU PSYCHOLOGY" is most applicable to the printed menu, although there are techniques that can be employed with *verbal* menus. However, the discussion here will be confined to the printed menu.

Some of the specific techniques employed in the design and production of a menu involve such elements as the use and selection of graphics; font style and size; gaze motion; primacy and recency; menu size and format; ink color; paper color, weight, texture, and finish; and cover material and design.

Even the placement of an item on a page or within a list is done for a reason. Actually, menu psychology techniques can be anything that directs the reader's attention to a particular area of the menu.

In a student study of an old Bennigan's

menu from the early 1980s, it was discovered that over three-fourths of all menu items sold were either snacks or appetizers. The menu had multiple pages, and the dinner entrées were listed on the last two pages. Apparently, customers didn't page through to the end, which resulted in fewer entrées being ordered.

Since menu psychology techniques are designed to get the patrons' attention, it is important to understand the way we typically "sight-in" on a menu. Studies using laser-light tracking have been able to monitor the eye movement across a menu. The way the eye moves across a menu has been described as "gaze motion." Given different menu formats — single fold-two panel, two fold-three panel, single page, etc. — different areas of sales concentration are noted.

It's important to note that gaze motion is not static. The eye can be drawn from the random gaze by the use of what I call "eye magnets," or those things that attract attention. Some of the best examples are graphic boxes that surround specific menu items; dot-matrix color screens used as backgrounds; larger or bolder type fonts; illustrations; and photographs. All of those techniques will draw the eye to a desired location. The areas of emphasis are where you should list the items you want to promote. Since the first grade when we were taught to read, we learned to begin reading at the upper left-hand side of a page. That is where we naturally will start unless eye magnets are created to attract our attention.

The menu format impacts the area of sales concentration

GAZE MOTION PATTERNS vary according to the page format, graphics, layout, and number of folds in the menu. Restaurants have a tendency to list items in the order in which they are consumed — in other words, appetizers come first, followed by salads, soups, entrées, vegetables and side dishes, and finally, desserts. How you organize your menu and where you place various items will impact their sales. Locating items in areas of sales concentrations increases the chances of their being sold.

A crowded menu that is difficult to read is not an effective merchandising tool. Restaurants with static menus that combine both lunch and dinner items can be quite extensive. And too many menus tend to be fairly large and crowded and use too small a type font. If a menu approaches 12 inches by 18 inches, mul-

> **"Tell me what you eat, and I will tell you what your are."**
>
> — JEAN ANTHELME BRILLAT-SAVARIN

---

tiple menus should be employed to keep the size manageable.

Separate drink, wine, dessert, and children's menus may be more practical and do a better merchandising job than one that is oversized and crowded. A separate dessert menu is a more effective sales piece than one that requires a customer to remember what was on the original menu. Table tents and menu boards can be used to merchandise daily specials when clip-ons add to the clutter and compete with the regular menu.

Menus are available in three basic types of page and fold formats. The first is the single-page format, which lists the entire menu on a single page or card. The area of sales concentration is on the top half of the page.

The most commonly used format is the two-page, single-fold menu. While size and shape vary, the National Restaurant Association reports that the most common size is 9 inches by 12 inches. That seems to be the result of nothing more mysterious than the fact that it accommodates the standard paper size of 8 1/2 inches by 11 inches.

The more extensive the number of listings, the larger the menu dimensions must be. But a menu that is larger than 13 inches by 18 inches when folded will be too large to read once it has been opened. Oversized menus are difficult to maneuver in tight quarters. I've seen wine glasses knocked over and menus scorched by lowboy candles. The area of greatest sales concentration on the two-page, single-fold menu is in the upper right-hand side when it is unfolded.

The third and perhaps most-popular format for moderately priced restaurants is the double-fold, three-panel menu. It provides six pages or panels for menu copy, utilizing both the front and back covers. The top two-thirds of the center panel is the area of greatest sales concentration. The three-panel look can be accomplished with a two-page, single-fold menu through the use of graphics or color-matrix screens.

The placement of menu items should be well planned and address your sales and cost objectives. Typically, entrées are accorded the greatest priority on the menu because they generate the greatest sales. However, consider the fact that virtually every customer orders an entrée, although not everyone orders an appetizer or a dessert.

If you're particularly proud of your appetizer, salad, and soup selections and want to sell more, give them priority placement on the menu. But don't forget that your entrées still must be prominently displayed, or you might encounter the same problems that Houlihan's and Bennigan's did with their old menu designs.

If you have a three-panel menu with inter-changeable pages, try swapping them at lunch and dinner for a month and then check your menu sales mix for any changes. Odds are that whatever is in the center panel will sell more than if it were on the back cover. That is also a way to increase your check average at night by moving your entrée selection to the center panel and the lower-priced sandwiches and salads to the back cover, where they're less likely to be noticed and therefore ordered.

13

A printed menu delivers a more consistent sales effort than a server can do verbally

THE PRINTED MENU has become the preferred method for presenting the items a restaurant prepares and serves well. While selling by servers can supplement the message, verbal menus have limited application for most popularly priced restaurants. Although I admit that we all can recall a particular server we've known or employed who could outsell any printed menu, such people are extremely rare. They possess a natural talent that cannot be taught or trained. Consequently, the printed menu is a safer bet.

Operators who have employed verbal menus in place of printed ones soon realize that they steal time from customer service. The time spent on recitation and question-and-answer follow-up can consume as much as 15 to 20 minutes — time that could and should be spent in addressing customer-service issues. Servers in general don't do an adequate job when it comes to describing and explaining the menu. Their presentations may range from monotone and indifference to highballing through the spiel to get on to more pressing matters. Furthermore, customers rarely pay absolute attention and are reluctant to ask that items be repeated. A printed menu placed before the customer can be reread as often as necessary.

Verbal descriptions have a place and serve an important role in upselling guests and reinforcing the printed menu. But verbal menus are not an alternative in themselves. A well-known West Coast restaurant relegated its verbal recitations to the slag heap of gastronomic history when it was discovered that upon returning to printed menus, the sales of the daily specials increased and the servers were freed to lavish even a greater level of service on guests.

14

Key components of menu design are texture, color, and weight of the paper; the style of type font; and ink color

THE AFOREMENTIONED ELEMENTS all contribute to the menu design and must be selected to complement the personality of the restaurant. Consider how we associate certain colors with certain types of restaurants. For example, Italian restaurants may use red-checkered tablecloths or napkins. Steak houses typically employ black and red in their booth upholstery, employee uniforms, and menu. Mexican restaurants utilize orange and yellow to a great extent. The menu cover, paper, ink, and even font style should communicate the personality of an operation.

Certain type fonts capture the style or personality of a particular concept. For example, compare Italian Restaurant with *Italian Restaurant*; **Silver Bullet Diner** and *Silver Bullet Diner*; ENGLISH PUB and English Pub; and Mexican

"Ability will never catch up with the demand for it."

— MALCOLM S. FORBES

Restaurant and **Mexican Restaurant**. Most would agree that the fonts in the second examples more appropriately express the personality of the various restaurant concepts. However, you should stay away from exotic type faces, script, and italic fonts. They can detract from graphics and illustrations used to draw the eye. If you must use them, use them sparingly and only for effect. Some examples of exotic type fonts that shouldn't be used on menus are *Pepita*, Narrowband, and american uncial. Note how much more difficult it is to read these fonts than to the rest of the text. As a rule, don't use more than three different styles of type; your menu will look cluttered and detract from the emphasis you might be seeking by using a certain type font for emphasis.

At least two-thirds of the menu should be set in lower-case letters because they are more readable in print than upper-case. UPPER-CASE, or CAPS, should be reserved for section titles, menu categories, and the name of the menu item. Since readability is the ultimate goal of the menu-production process, you must select font sizes that fit the available space without being too small or too crowded.

A common fault in design is to reduce the size of the type font and crowd the items if a menu is too small. That reduces the effectiveness of the design, making it difficult to read under low-light conditions. The smallest type font used on a menu should be 12 points. That is the default font size on your computer.

Leave an adequate amount of space — or leading — between printed lines. Leading is measured in points, and a minimum of three-point *leading* is preferred for ease of reading. The space between individual letters can be adjusted as well. Space can be added through a process called *kerning*, which moves the letters closer together. Space between letters also can be increased through a process called *letter spacing*. If parts of the menu are duplicated, typed, or otherwise produced in-house, use an ink-jet or laser printer.

Ink and paper color must be selected for readability and design consideration. A multiple-color menu can be produced inexpensively (compared with full-color printing) by selecting different ink and paper colors. Colors must contrast yet complement the color scheme of a restaurant's interior, table-top, and employee uniforms. Two or three colors can be as effective as a full-color menu. Although black ink on white paper provides the best contrast, tinted paper and tinted inks also can be effective and inexpensive to use. The use of dot-matrix screens can take an ink color — red, for example — and provide a range of colors from a pale red blush or pink to a deep red used in a border. The 10-percent-to-20-percent screens of color can be overprinted in black and produce a nice contrast that will help items stand out.

Paper texture, weight, and finish also can add character to a menu and help communicate the personality of the restaurant. The weight of the interior pages typically is lighter than that of the cover stock. Paper texture can be made to resemble wood, leather, velvet, or suede. The rough textures are great for effect but soil easily and aren't as durable as smooth-textured coated paper. Paper opacity is important when you're printing on both sides, and you don't want the ink to bleed through. Paper can be coated with high- or low-gloss finish to prolong its life. Porous papers can be laminated with plastic, although such treatment doesn't fit the personality of most white-tablecloth restaurants. Uncoated papers laminate best. Many new, synthetic materials are being used in place of laminated papers that are waterproof and tear-resistant and are available in a wide range of colors.

Menu-sales-mix analysis can provide insight into product- and worker-flow efficiency in the kitchen

EFFICIENT KITCHENS DON'T HAPPEN unless the menu first has been coordinated with the equipment selection and layout. Achieving the desired average check and total gross profit do not happen by chance, either. Is your kitchen inefficient in sending out orders in a steady and timely manner? Do certain stations "crash" on busy nights when you need them most, causing delays in service and mistakes with food orders? Is your average food check lower than it should be? Is your overall gross profit return short of your expectations?

If you answered yes to those questions and feel that fundamentally you have a better-than-average cost-control program, the culprit probably is your menu design. Yes, I said menu design. Remember: Regardless of the design, if a menu is used on a regular basis, a predictable sales mix inevitably will result. Since that occurs with any menu format and design, you must design your menu to achieve revenue and profit objectives.

If the kitchen is slow in getting out the food during busy periods, examine the kitchen stations that are being hit the hardest. Begin by matching each menu item to the station or individuals in the kitchen who "touch" that item during its preparation for service. You can monitor the product flow from the time that ingredients are removed from refrigeration to the time the completed plate is delivered to the pick-up window. Note how many different employees handle it. If more than two people are required to turn out a single item, the preparation must be simplified.

You also should monitor the worker flow between various pieces of equipment. The kitchen staff must have everything it needs within a work area of 10 linear feet. If staffers are walking more than three or four steps to obtain ingredients and utensils, they're traveling too much. And if you find that half of the menu items sent out during a peak period are being prepared at one station or by one individual, rearrange equipment to distribute some of the orders to other stations.

Sometimes that means repositioning certain pieces of equipment so that another station can take a greater share of the orders. If you own, manage, or have worked in a short-order kitchen, you can appreciate my point. But with all of that having been said, I still cannot overstate the importance of the menu design in making the kitchen run more smoothly and efficiently.

16

KEY

The menu design impacts the average check and the gross-profit return on each sale

HOW MUCH THE TYPICAL customer spends in your restaurant is a critical statistic. An operator should know how much daily sales must be to break even. In addition, a daily sales goal should be set that can help to achieve an operation's profit objectives.

For example, if you determine that the daily sales average must be $1,800 to cover expenses and overhead and still return an 8-percent profit, and that you can expect to serve 180 covers each day (assuming one meal period per day for this example), your average check must be $10.00 per customer.

If your customer counts are fairly predictable, and a regular pattern of customer traffic allows you to forecast labor schedules and purchase and prepare in the correct quantities, your main objective will be to convince those customers to spend at least $10.00 each time they visit your restaurant. The amount they spend will determine not only your check average but also the gross-profit return on each sale. Your menu prices and design must be established in relation to the average check and resulting gross-profit return.

When you must achieve a check average of $10.00 per person, your menu should not place items selling for less than $8.95 in the areas of sales emphasis. Furthermore, type styles and sizes and other graphic techniques used to draw the customer's attention should be reserved for menu items priced at $9.95 and above. If you have more than 25 percent to 33 percent of your entrées priced below $8.95, and they happen to be popular items, you will likely find that your check average falls beneath your $10.00 target.

If your menu design is not emphasizing the items priced to generate your desired check average, the only way you can achieve the average is by selling add-on items like appetizers and desserts. However, I recommend that since less than half of your customers will order either an appetizer or a dessert, you will need to feature items priced at and above $9.95. That greatly increases the likelihood a customer will spend at least $9.95. Consequently, the sale of appetizers and desserts will result in a check average greater than your $10.00 goal.

Utilize the theory of 'primacy and recency' in your menu design

THE THEORY OF "PRIMACY AND RECENCY" is a psychological concept that asserts that people are more likely to remember the first or last thing they read or heard.

That theory can be applied to the psychology of menu design by placing the items we most want to sell in places they are likely to be seen first or last. Particular locations in each menu format are designated as areas of sales emphasis. The assumption is that if an item is placed in one of those locations, the customer will be prompted to remember it and, consequently, order it rather than something else.

The theory of primacy and recency also is demonstrated in the order in which items are listed in a column on a menu. If you offer 10 menu selections, it's better to position them in two lists of five rather than one list of 10

> **"To get what you want, STOP doing what isn't working."**
>
> — DENNIS WEAVER

---

because you will have more opportunities to emphasis key menu items. Two lists will produce twice the number of items that will be remembered.

Perhaps you've seen the television infomercial hosted by comedian John Ritter in which a "Professor Olney" expounds on his method to improve your memory or ability to retain more information when you are studying for exams. He begins the show by calling out a series of numbers and then asks the audience to write down the ones they remember. The majority recall the first and last numbers called out. That exercise serves to demonstrate that when a server verbally recites a menu to the guest, the items mentioned first and last should be the ones management wants to emphasize.

Primacy and recency also can be used to *de-emphasize* certain items that may have high food costs or are labor intensive. Place such items in the middle of a list where they are, for practical purposes, "hidden." Remember: The theory of primacy and recency says that if you can recall an item, it will be ordered more often than ordinary random chance would permit.

The effect that menu design can have on a customer's choice was illustrated to me once when a sales representative from a local radio station paid a sales call at my restaurant. He proposed a series of 30-second ads that I could afford and offered to produce sample spots for my approval. The only thing he required was my menu. When he returned a few weeks later and played the spots, I was impressed with their production quality. But I asked him to change the items that had been featured in the ads. The menu items he had mentioned were high in food cost and labor intensive — certainly not the dishes I wanted to sell more than others. I instructed him which items to showcase as specialties of the house, and we signed the agreement for the radio spots.

It was after I sold my restaurants that I learned about the theory of primacy and recency, and that incident immediately came to mind. I questioned whether my menu had been communicating to the customer what the copywriter from the radio station had gleaned from it. The answer was probably yes, because I had never compiled that menu with any ideas about which items I wanted to emphasize.

The next time you visit the drive-through window at McDonald's or Wendy's, be conscious of what draws your eye first. If it's just a list of menu items and prices, note which of the items have been listed first and last. You will probably find that it is one of their "featured" sandwiches.

And have you ever noticed that the large-size beverage is listed first? That technique is meant to get you to "upsize" your drink and spend 25 cents more. Thus, once you've realized that the forces of primacy and recency are at work, regardless of how your menu is designed, why not put them to use to sell the items you choose rather than just leaving sales to chance?

18

The cover design should incorporate elements of menu psychology

TRADITIONALLY, THE COVER of a menu contains the name of the restaurant and a logo. The logo and color scheme is carried over into signage, matchbooks, cocktail napkins, guest checks, print advertising, and letterhead. That use of the common logo and color on the menu and other printed matter is referred to as *thematic continuity.* Thus, when the public sees those items, they reinforce the identity of the restaurant.

Today, however, some menus don't have recognizable covers; instead, the covers list appetizers and cocktails — utilizing the theory of primacy and recency, I suspect. In other cases, covers contain elaborate illustrations of the restaurant's exterior or local landmarks associated with the operation's personality. The East Bay Trading Company Restaurant in

> **"Worry about being better; bigger will take care of itself. Think one customer at a time and take care of each one the best way you can."**
>
> — GARY COMER

Charleston, S.C., features a drawing of its historical building and restaurant on the cover. The Ritz-Carlton Buckhead in Atlanta used a water color painting of the restaurant exterior. Often the back cover is left completely blank, which is a waste because additional information could be included with only a slight increase in production costs.

I'm amazed at the number of restaurants that don't include their address, telephone number, and hours of operation on the menu. I guess they assume that everyone knows where they're located because they are seated in the restaurant. I recommend that such information be included somewhere on the menu.

Covers can be separate from the internal pages that contain the menu-item listings or are self-contained on a single page. The material used should be determined by the length of time the menu will be in service and the conditions of moisture and food soilage it will be subjected to while in use. Menus for coffee shops and family restaurants do not normally have separate covers and must use materials that are water and grease resistant. Mylar lamination is used to protect the menu. At the very least, coated-paper stocks are used on menu covers.

Fine-dining menus are not subject to such conditions and are usually two-part formats with a separate permanent cover and an interchangeable interior section printed on parchmentlike paper. Plastic covers or lamination would not fit the personality and image of a white-tablecloth operation. The cover often is made of a durable faux leather or vinyl. However, uncoated paper also can be used, as handling by the guest in a fine-dining environment is greatly reduced.

Menu covers for moderately priced theme restaurants are often just panels slipped into a plastic menu cover or printed on synthetic materials that are water- and tear-resistant. The three-panel, two-fold style is the most common format and provides great flexibility where panels must be changed independently of the rest of the menu. That type of format also offers significant opportunities to test for primacy-and recency-influence by changing the location of the menu panel inserts.

(1) The ideal menu items to emphasize in your menu design are the ones that are popular, low in food cost, and return the highest total gross profit.

    A. True
    B. False

(2) Weighted gross profit is actually more relevant than individual gross profit.

    A. True
    B. False

(3) Which items in cost-margin analysis are the menu items that are popular, low in food cost and return a high weighted contribution margin?

    A. Standards
    B. Problems
    C. Primes
    D. Sleepers

(4) What would be the best strategy for dealing with a "Sleeper" item on your menu?

    A. Lower the price and make it a "special"
    B. Increase the portion size
    C. Place it in a prominent location on the menu
    D. All of the above

(5) All "Problems" should be removed from the menu.

    A. True
    B. False

ANSWERS: 1: A, 2: A, 3: C, 4: D, 5: B

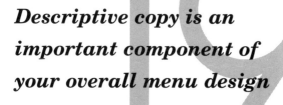

Descriptive copy is an important component of your overall menu design

SINCE THE MENU is the only piece of printed matter a restaurant produces that is guaranteed to be read by every adult customer, menu copy is a critical component in the overall menu design. Menu copy should describe the menu items in such a way that the words paint a picture and taste expectation.

Copywriting is important in all advertising, not just menu descriptions. Because of the high costs of advertising during prime time on television and in popular newspapers and magazines, creative copywriters are paid to paint images with their words that will be recalled long after the television has been shut off or a magazine tossed out. We all recall the classic words of past advertising campaigns like Wendy's "Where's the beef?"; Burger King's "Have it your way"; Coca Cola's "The Real

Thing"; and KFC's "We do chicken right."

Menu copy describes the menu items, promotes the restaurant, and tells customers what the restaurant is selling. There are four categories of menu copy. The first is the *menu category*: appetizers, salads, entrées, desserts, etc. The second is the *name of the menu item*: top sirloin steak, broiled red snapper, or quarter pounder. The third category is the *descriptive copy* that lists the ingredients, preparation method, and accompaniments. The fourth is referred to as *institutional copy*, which includes such general information about the operation as ownership, historical significance of the name or location, address, hours of operation, and the like.

The most important of the four concerns the descriptions of the menu items themselves. There are two schools of thought on how descriptive copy should be written. One emphasizes brevity, while the other utilizes long, flowery wording that stretches literal descriptions. Where menu descriptions are concerned, it's important not to confuse "cute" with "creative." When you give menu items clever or cute names, like calling a deli sandwich the "Woody Allen," the accompanying descriptive copy is essential because the item cannot be identified from the name alone. So your menu must tell customers that the Woody Allen is "sliced breast of smoked turkey, Swiss cheese, and pastrami, fresh marinated mushrooms, and our own Bermuda onion spread on Jewish marble rye."

Having to read lengthy menu copy slows down the order-taking process, and the specific merchandising effect can be lost amid the volume of printed words — especially if the menu contains more than six printed pages. Just as a writer for a situation comedy must place the lines of dialogue within a specific situation and in the context of a particular character, the menu copywriter must match the copy to the operation and concept. In other words, what works well for an operation like Ed Debevic's in Chicago will not work for a diner operation in Atlanta. Menu copy is only one part of the total menu design and must build upon the servers, the location, and customer expectations. Descriptive menu copy is just one element that customers use in building their overall impression of a restaurant.

Generally, the following information is covered in the descriptive copy:

(1) The method of preparation, such as broiled, pan-fried, grilled, etc.

(2) The essential or main ingredients if they are unusual or unique to your restaurant. That does not mean that you have to list every ingredient in the recipe.

(3) The way the item is served and its accompaniments, such as served *en casserole with rice pilaf and steamed asparagus*.

(4) Quality claims, such as the grade or freshness of the ingredients.

(5) The variety or geographic origin: Alaskan king crab, Smithfield ham, or Black Angus prime beef.

If you use a menu name that is commonly recognized, you don't need to describe how the item is prepared. The menu copy for a steak item may indicate the grade: USDA Choice; geographic origin: Iowa corn-fed; and specific breed: Certified Black Angus and mesquite-broiled. Adding "broiled to perfection" or "cooked to the degree of doneness that cuts with a fork" is unnecessary.

Using foreign words to sell an item is fine, but care must be taken to provide an explanation if the phrase or description is not self-explanatory. Florence Fabricant, contributing writer to Nation's Restaurant News, has researched trends in menu copywriting and suggests that menu descriptions are often unintentionally misleading to the diner because of to the inclusion of "fusion cuisine" menu items. Regional cooking has been combined with ethnic recipes resulting in the coining of terms or the usage of classic French terms incorrectly. The Escoffier school of French cooking will stick to the classic meaning of menu descriptions; however, the term Caesar salad doesn't necessarily guarantee that the customer will receive the classic version. Paul Prudhomme's famous blackened redfish is an example of how a regional dish can be copied by competitors and how the preparation can vary depending on the restaurant and its location.

20

Remember: The purpose of descriptive copy is to sell, not to confuse the reader

DESCRIPTIVE COPY used on menus and in advertising is being scrutinized more closely than ever before for misrepresentations. Truth in menu is an obligation of the restaurant owner and chef. The customer must be presented with an accurate description of the item, and if we, as restaurant operators, do not comply voluntarily, expect state and federal laws to be passed to protect the public. Misrepresentation of ingredients, grades, brands, varieties, and geographical origin are fraudulent advertising.

So don't say an item is fresh if it has been frozen; don't describe it as imported if domestic ingredients were used; and don't overstate portion weights or counts. Merchandising claims are a gray area for descriptive menu copy. If there's any place for poetic license, it is in merchandising copy. Statements such as "the best

"Anybody can cut prices, but it takes brains to produce a better article."

— P. D. ARMOUR

Italian restaurant in town," or "our service is second to none," or "authentic Oriental cooking" are basically unsubstantiated and boastful statements that are both difficult to prove or dispute.

One must be careful with "color" words used in menu descriptions. Truth-in-menu guidelines prohibit such claims as "home-made," "farm-fresh," "garden-fresh," "dry-aged," or "made with butter" unless the items meet the established standards for such descriptions. Review your menu copy for such excessive literary license used by your copywriter.

Menu copy should describe the item clearly and succinctly. Phrases rather than complete sentences are recommended. If color words are used, be certain they're "food-associated" words. Some menu copy reads as if the writer consulted a thesaurus to locate the most complicated synonyms. Words like majestic, embraced, and sensuous are not words used to describe sauces and desserts. Avoid the use of terms like drenched, mounds, smothered, and the overused "cooked to perfection" or "cooked to your specifications."

Consider a Reuben sandwich described as "a pile of tender corned beef smothered under a mound of sauerkraut, covered with a thick layer of melted Swiss Cheese, and topped with a dollop of homemade Thousand Island dressing on grilled Pumpernickel bread." That might be considered overselling. A more moderate approach might read, "Warm and tender sliced corned beef brisket, a touch of sauerkraut, imported big eye Swiss cheese, homemade Thousand Island dressing on dark Pumpernickel bread, grilled and served with a Kosher pickle half."

Don't confuse the issue with your descriptive copy. An overdescription can turn a simple menu item into a chaos of sauces and ingredients. Remember: You're not giving someone the recipe. If the main ingredients in your Chicken Cacciatore are baked chicken, green peppers, onions, and mushrooms in a rich tomato sauce with a touch of Marsala wine, say just that. You don't need to list the spices and seasonings.

(1) Any menu, any design, or any menu format will produce a predictable menu-sales mix if put into service every day for a prolonged period of time.

    A. True
    B. False

(2) Menu design actually can turn unpopular menu items into top sellers, regardless of what they are.

    A. True
    B. False

(3) The technique of menu design used to turn an ordinary menu into a merchandising and cost-control tool is referred to as:

    A. Menu engineering
    B. Menu psychology
    C. Cost/margin Analysis
    D. Value pricing

(4) Which of the following is not a technique used in menu design?

    A. Eye magnets
    B. Ink color
    C. Type font (style)
    D. None of the above

(5) The area of sales concentration on a menu will vary with the number of folds, pages and panels.

    A. True
    B. False

ANSWERS: 1: A, 2: B, 3: B, 4: D, 5: A

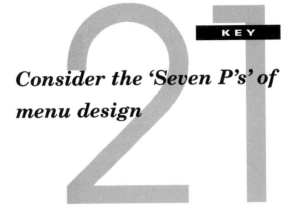

Consider the 'Seven P's' of menu design

MARKETING THEORY has the "Four P's," consisting of Promotion, Place, Price, and Product. We can apply the same theory to the role of the menu in marketing. Through menu design we can influence the sales mix of menu items by utilizing related techniques.

The "Seven P's" of menu design are as follows:

(1) Purchase price
(2) Portioning/packaging
(3) Positioning
(4) Promotion
(5) Product
(6) Price
(7) Place

> **"If the only tool you have is a hammer, you tend to see every problem as a nail."**
>
> — ABRAHAM MASLOW

Those factors can be used to alter the sales mix when you're seeking to achieve a particular goal, such as lowering the food cost, raising the average check, or increasing gross profit return.

The purchase price refers to what you are paying for the ingredients used in each recipe. If you emphasize quality, you likely will pay a higher price. If your menu descriptions indicate high-quality grades — Prime, Fancy, or Grade A, for example — high standards are communicated to the customer, a strategy that can provide your restaurant with a competitive edge over those who serve average quality.

Portioning and packaging are two more elements that can be used to communicate value when you are marketing particular menu items. Further emphasis can be drawn to menu items by adding or deleting accompaniments or by providing larger portions. The accompaniments that are served with each entrée or sandwich offer a way to "package" the item much the same way retailers package products and services together. Another name for packaging is "bundling." A fast-food operation bundles the sandwich, fries and beverage and calls it a "value meal deal."

In tableservice operations packaging refers to the product presentation as well as the accompaniments. The proper selection of flatware and garnitures will enhance the visual presentation of the product and increase the likelihood that a customer will order it. We make our ordering decisions based more often on how an item looks than how it tastes. In essence, we first eat with our eyes. Packaging also refers to such dining-room amenities as table linens, candles, flowers, and tableside preparation and plating.

Positioning refers to the location of the item on the menu. The use of primacy and recency and gaze motion will improve the likelihood of selection by the customer.

Promotion refers to anything that is done to draw attention to a specific menu item in order to improve its chance of being ordered. In addition to our regular printed menu, we can supplement our marketing efforts with table tents, menu boards, and clip-on menu cards. On the regular menu we employ graphics and color screens to ensure that parts of the menu stand out from the rest.

Product refers to doing something so unique that it is transformed from an ordinary commodity into a specialty good. If you have a specialty good, you have, in essence, a monopoly on that item. That distinction not only provides your operation with a competitive edge but also allows you the privileges that go along with having a monopoly. In fact, you can charge what the market will bear.

The price you charge certainly can influence selection by the customer. However, discounting or low price leaders is not the recommended way to build an image of quality and high standards.

Place pertains to how the product can be obtained by the consumer. In a table-service or fast-food operation, the customer must enter the building. If a drive-through window is provided, the customer doesn't even have to leave the car to order. Delivery brings the food to the customers instead of requiring them to come to the food. Operations seeking to make it more convenient for the consumer to make a purchase offer such "place" alternatives as home delivery, carry-out, off-premise, catering, picnic lunches, and special events.

Limited versus extensive menus? How many items should a menu contain?

A menu is sometimes described as being limited or extensive. Those adjectives are used to describe not only the actual number of menu items but also the different ways in which the items are prepared and served.

Operators limit the number of menu items to help control production costs and decrease inventory. A limited menu reduces equipment requirements, kitchen space, and labor costs. On the other hand, menus are expanded primarily to broaden customer appeal, in much the same way that steak houses add chicken or seafood dishes.

Fast-food restaurants typically have limited the number of menu items to maintain quality and limit the preparation methods to simplify production. Such operations feature "limited-limited" menus — in other words, fewer items prepared only one way. However, even fast-food chains have been forced to increase the number and variety of menus items over the years. Take McDonald's, KFC, Arby's, and Burger King as examples. Not only do they introduce new items to broaden their customer base and bring regulars back more often, but they also cobrand with other limited menu concepts.

Coffee-shop restaurants like Denny's and IHOP that serve breakfast, lunch, and dinner offer a rather extensive list of menu choices. But by limiting the number of ways the items are prepared, they can manage production and reduce the number of items they carry in inventory. Their menus are therefore "extensive-limited" — extensive in terms of choices but limited in methods of preparation. But those types of restaurants have also expanded their menus by simply combining existing ingredients to create new menu items. Consider how the same chicken breast can be used in a sandwich, on a diet platter, in a salad, or as an entrée.

Casual-theme or specialty restaurants have utilized the technique of taking a limited number of main dishes and designing the menu to appear to offer extensive choices. By preparing and combining ingredients in different ways, they have developed a menu that appears to offer many choices but is manageable from the perspectives of production, inventory, and cost controls. Those menus are "limited-extensive" — limited in terms of ingredients but extensive in terms of preparation methods. For example, one menu might use 12-to-15-count headless shrimp in shrimp cocktail, shrimp scampi, Cajun-spiced grilled shrimp, shrimp fajitas, and batter-fried shrimp. The addition of a few inexpensive ingredients results in five ways to list shrimp on the menu.

The ubiquitous hamburger can be ordered with several different toppings, including a choice of cheeses, mushrooms, bacon, and ham, creating an extensive number of choices with even a variety of buns. Being a former owner-operator of two Italian restaurants, I learned firsthand that pasta dishes served with a variety of sauces can create a rather extensive list of choices for the customer. We advertised "23 menu items under $5." The restaurant offered five different sauces — marinara, ground beef, meatball, sausage, and clam — served over spaghettini, penne, lasagna, manicotti, and linguine. The five sauces and five pastas allowed us to make our menu appear extensive but let us still control quality, cost, and production.

The final group is the fine-dining restaurants that feature an extensive number of menu items offered in a variety of preparation methods. Those menus are termed "extensive-extensive." Usually, a menu of that type is found in a resort or convention hotel, chef-owned independent restaurant, or a private club and requires a knowledgeable and skilled culinary staff to produce. Fine-dining restaurants rarely have static menus — menus that basically remain the same except for a few seasonal changes from month to month.

The American diner has shown that he or she can consume large quantities of chicken, pasta, steak, pizza, and Italian food — and eat it more than one night a week. Despite that, restaurant menus must change both to keep the

> **"An empowered organization is one in which individuals have the knowledge, skill, desire, and opportunity to personally succeed in a way that leads to collective organizational success."**
>
> — STEPHEN R. COVEY

---

adventurous diner coming back and to attract new customers.

That begs the question, "How many items should a menu contain? It's a given that the more items you list on your menu, the more difficult the menu is to manage in terms of food cost and quality control; the greater number of items you must purchase and keep in inventory; the more equipment and space you will need; the more skilled your kitchen staff must be; and the more difficult it will be to forecast orders and preparation quantities. Therefore, you should attempt to limit the menu to a *manageable* number without limiting the choices to your customers.

Time and time again, menu-sales analysis of the most popular-selling entrées (and this holds true for other menu categories as well) will disclose that 60 percent to 75 percent of the items sold are the same eight to 12 selections.

In the case of other menu categories with proportionally fewer choices on the menu, 60 percent of the sales will come from approximately half of the choices in each category. What that means is that of 400 entrées sold on a given night, 240 to 300 are those eight to 12 items. That will occur regardless of whether there are 48 or 24 choices. You should question the benefits of offering so many choices when some items sell only two or three orders per week — especially if the ingredients are used only in that menu item.

It would appear, therefore, that most menus shouldn't require any more than 18 to 24 entrée selections. The actual number will vary depending on the type of restaurant concept, the number of seats, and the meal periods served. But why should you carry additional items on the menu that simply take up inventory space and make quality and cost control more difficult? Sales analysis will reveal unpopular menu items and the folly of a menu that is overly extensive. Consider that variety is not defined by the number of choices you provide, but by the acceptability of those choices.

(1) The term "packaging" in menu design refers to:

    A. Product presentation
    B. The flatware and garniture
    C. The entrée accompaniments
    D. All of the above

(2) The terms "limited" and "extensive," as they apply to menu offerings, refer only to the number of menu selections listed on the menu.

    A. True
    B. False

(3) Which is an example of a "limited/extensive" menu?

    A. A coffee shop like Denny's or IHOP
    B. A specialty restaurant like Red Lobster
    C. A fast-food restaurant
    D. A fine-dining restaurant

(4) Children's menus should target kids under the age of 10.

    A. True
    B. False

(5) Which of the following is not a common menu mistake?

    A. Aligning prices in a straight column
    B. Using too small a type font
    C. Breaking the page into two columns
    D. Using exotic and script fonts

ANSWERS: 1: D, 2: B, 3: B, 4: A, 5: C

If you want to attract more families, offer a separate children's menu

WHY SHOULD YOU CONCERN yourself with satisfying children with a special menu? The reason is that studies conducted by national restaurant chains and such professional associations as the National Restaurant Association have reported that children play a major role in eating-out decisions. The children's market, estimated at between 1.7 million and 2 million under the age of 10, is obviously a market segment worth pursuing.

Children's menus pose a challenge to the menu designer. First, an operator must include food items that are preferred by kids between the ages of 3 and 10 years old, priced low enough to encourage families to dine there, and present the menu in a playful and entertaining way. If you operate a family restaurant, your menu already offers food for children. It may be

> **"He that waits upon fortune is never sure of a dinner."**
>
> — BENJAMIN FRANKLIN

---

in the form of a small but separate section on the regular menu that contains three or four items at a lower price. Or it could be a separate children's menu that has some entertainment value, such as a game or puzzle.

In her excellent book, *Kids Dine Out*, Susan Gilleran reports that 55 percent of parents said their kids influence the decision to dine at a table-service restaurant, while 47 percent said their kids determined the specific restaurant. Apparently, courting kids is one way of attracting families. But children today are smarter, more worldly, and more independent than kids were 30 years ago. Therefore, those of us who are over 30 need to add two or three years to the actual age of children to allow for this "worldly" stature.

We used to think of children as *those under 12 years of age*. But 11- and 12-year-old boys and girls won't order from a separate children's menu. Instead, they order from the adult menu and get appetizers and side orders, if not full adult entrées. Consequently, the children's menu must target kids under the age of 10. However, keep in mind that the foods that will satisfy a 10-year old are not the same foods that a 5-year old will eat, and vice versa. At the same time you should remember that the younger the kids, the shorter their attention span and ability to sit still with nothing but a napkin and silverware to occupy their hands.

The age difference also impacts the complexity of the games and puzzles you include on your children's menus. While a toddler will scribble on a place mat and be content, older kids need greater challenges. Girls and boys will have different interests, so the theme of the games must address gender as well as age.

A place-mat menu with games is effective in occupying time while the food is being prepared. Crayons are provided so that the kids can color or work the puzzles. Speed of service, child-sized portions, and reasonable prices are important to parents. Some independents and chains have offered to feed children at no charge during certain hours of the week; others price children's portions at cost. The same item served to an adult should be three times the menu price for the kid's portion. That is done solely for marketing purposes. Unfortunately, one drawback is that it's often difficult to explain to the older lady or gentleman who wants to order from the children's menu and pay the same price.

Another way operators can justify charging low prices for kids' meals is that there are only two sources of new customers: those who formerly ate at a competing operation and those who are nurtured as children. As to pricing children's meals, Gilleran offers some creative suggestions. One alternative to pricing at cost is to have children pay what they weigh.

Keep a scale handy so that kids can weigh themselves. If a kid weighs 45 pounds, he or she pays 45 cents. Another suggestion is to charge them their age times 25 cents or 50 cents. Or you can offer two free children's meals up to a value of $2.50 each for each adult dinner purchased.

Lastly, to really please children, the food must be fun to eat. That can be accomplished without much additional cost. Fun foods are those that can be eaten with the fingers, and you can make them more attractive by cutting them into different shapes, like stars, hearts, or animals. That works well for chicken nuggets, fish sticks, and pizza toppings. Consider using different pasta shapes instead of ordinary spaghetti or penne also. Or cut sandwiches into small geometric shapes with cookie cutters.

Remember: The purpose of a children's menu is to make it fun for the kids to eat in your restaurant. If they enjoy themselves, they'll want to return. And to do that, they have to bring their parents. Special toys or gifts are another effective way to attract children, as evidenced by the movie-related promotions conducted by all of the major fast-food chains.

Gilleran makes the interesting observation that the influence of children on where their parents take them to eat is driven, at least in part, by guilt. Working parents don't want to deny their children, and the evening meal is the only time they have to get together, share news, and bond. The decision on what and where to eat often is left to the kids. It's a market worth exploring.

24

If you want to sell more wine and desserts, design separate menus for each

THE CONCEPT OF FEATURING separate wine and dessert menus is based on the theory that if the customer reads them, he or she at least will consider the purchase decision — hence, the likelihood of a sale is increased. Most wine purchases made with dinner are not impulse purchases; they're usually made by patrons who appreciate how a good wine enhances the entire dining experience. But if the menu contains a familiar brand name or favorite wine and is priced appropriately for the concept, even those customers who don't ordinarily order wine may be inclined to make a purchase. In other words you can increase the odds that someone will order a glass or bottle of wine by simply putting it on the menu. And the same holds true for desserts.

Certainly, you can include both your wine and dessert choices on the same menu that lists

> **"The ability to deal with people is as purchasable a commodity as sugar or coffee. And I pay more for that ability than for any other under the sun."**
>
> — JOHN D. ROCKEFELLER

---

your appetizers, salads, side dishes, and entrées. But if you have an extensive wine list and want to avoid crowding, the menu dimensions might have to be increased to accommodate the selections. On the other hand, if desserts are relegated to a small section near the end of the menu, the effectiveness of the menu copy is greatly diminished. So if you want to sell more wines and desserts, provide a prominent location on the menu for them and supplement it with suggestive selling by the server.

Another approach is to provide separate menus for cocktails, wines, after-dinner drinks, and desserts. If your wine list is longer than one page, it should be given its own menu, unless you are using a menu format that can accommodate it, such as a three-panel, two-fold menu. Whatever your menu decision, though, every wine list must be coordinated with the food menu. Some menus even suggest a wine with each menu offering.

Price your wines reasonably. With customers becoming more sophisticated, they often can recognize when a wine has been overpriced. If the average price for a full bottle is higher than double that of your average entrée price, your wine list should include several selections that are priced less. Wines should be offered by the bottle, half bottle, carafe, half carafe, and glass to appeal to a broader customer base.

Descriptive copy should explain whether the wine is slightly sweet, semi-dry, fruity, light, crisp, or robust, as well as what kinds of foods it complements. For example, "broiled marinated duck breast with cassis pecan brown butter with '97 Charles Shaw Gamay Beaujolais" or "spaghetti with pancetta and onion sauce with '97 Ravenswood Zinfandel."

Many progressive restaurants offer a reserve wine list of older vintages for the true wine aficionados. The task of merchandising wines to the casual wine drinker is to remove the "fear factor" in ordering wine. The customer can select a wine with confidence if you supply some "easy-to-pronounce" descriptive terms — perhaps a glossary of phonetic pronunciations — or recommend particular wines with specific courses or entrées.

A common way to prepare an attractive wine list is to place the bottle labels in a binder. With many customers limiting their consumption of liquor, a glass of wine often is ordered instead of a before-dinner cocktail. Increasingly, you find drink lists being employed, with the first page and covers of menus now being used to list before-dinner drinks. At the same time the dessert menu may include specialty after-dinner drinks prepared with espresso or ice cream. Those drinks are targeted at the casual drinkers, not the brandy and cognac connoisseurs.

Desserts are probably the easiest menu item to sell. They are largely an impulse item, and the likelihood of making a sale increases in proportion to the amount of visual content employed. Straight, verbal description is about 50-percent less effective than the sight of a full-color photograph of the dessert or specialty drink. Many restaurateurs who seek to increase dessert sales have produced full-color menus complete with photographs. Others use a display tray that is brought to the table. Restaurants like the Peasant Corporation's Dailey's in Atlanta have a dessert bar that is a focal point of the dining room. The percentage of parties not ordering a dessert after viewing the beautiful selections is low. And Dailey's dessert prices are about half what the average entrée costs, so they contribute significantly to overall sales.

KEY

Avoid the most common menu design mistakes

IF A RESTAURANT IS FINANCIALLY successful, one could argue that the menu has contributed to its success. We know that the menu offerings play a key role in an operation's success. The menu must offer items that its clientele want at prices they are willing to pay. However, most menus don't optimize the cost-control, communications, and marketing benefits because of some common menu mistakes. If those mistakes are addressed, the menu will become more effective in helping you achieve your goals.

Too often the size and format of a menu is selected based on convenience. It's not surprising that the most common size and format is the 9-inch-by-12-inch single-fold, two-page menu; that's the size that accommodates the standard 8.5-inch-by-11-inch sheet of paper. But

> **"Quality is remembered long after the price is forgotten."**
>
> — GUCCI FAMILY SLOGAN

---

that doesn't mean that it is the most effective size and format.

We often begin our research on menu design by collecting and reviewing existing menus from similar restaurants. We note which menu items have been listed and the menu design that has been chosen. We then conclude that if three out of four restaurants list an item on their menus or employ a particular design, it must be the thing to do. What we fail to realize is that they may have decided on their menu design and format in the same manner. The error is that we interpret the industry norm as the right thing to do. But in essence it's simply the blind leading the blind. I'm not claiming that the format of a particular menu may be an error; I'm just saying that the way we go about deciding on the content and format is flawed.

Another common mistake is to design the page as if one were typing a letter. Many operators begin on the left side with the name of the dish. Then they add the menu description followed by a line of dots that runs across the width of the page and ends at the price. Consequently, the customer sees the prices in the right margin and the names of the menu items in the left. Why not break the page into two columns? Utilize the power of "primacy and recency" when listing your items on a page.

Other common mistakes include crowding a menu with descriptive copy and utilizing a type font that's too small to read under low-light conditions. Those mistakes often occur because the size of the menu has been determined before the menu is typeset. As a result, the printer must reduce the type font to fit the space. If you have decided to offer an extensive menu, you either must increase its dimensions or go to separate menus for meal periods, desserts, or wine lists. Remember: Don't design a menu that requires copy printed in anything smaller than 12-point type.

The value of well-written descriptive copy is often lost on many menus. While long and flowery phrases are sometimes criticized, it is also a flaw not to utilize any descriptive copy at all. The standard menu items like steaks, chicken, and salads often are "underdescribed" on a menu. Consider a menu offering "Sirloin Steak, $9.95." Is the customer to assume that it is broiled as opposed to grilled? What grade of meat is used? What is included with the steak? If the restaurant purchases only corn-fed Iowa beef, shouldn't that be stated on the menu? If a special wood-burning char-broiler is used, shouldn't that be mentioned? If an operation is relying on verbal descriptions from the servers, an inconsistent and incomplete description can result.

When the layout of the menu is left to the printer, a completely balanced menu is often the result. The problem with a balanced layout that utilizes common menu headings, font sizes, and styles is that every item is treated equally. And when every item is accorded equal treatment and emphasis on the menu, nothing stands out. The items you want to sell the most must be given different treatment and emphasis. And that is accomplished through the use of various techniques to catch the attention of the reader, such as graphics, dot-matrix screens, and bolder and larger type.

Many operations offering daily specials that must be placed on menu clip-ons often haven't planned their menus well. As often as not, the clip-ons end up covering existing menu items, and few customers look to see what is underneath. As a result, sales of the obscured item suffer. If daily specials are a regular part of your menu, design a special place for them where they won't hide other food items you want to sell.

The final common menu mistake I've found is that many operators use type fonts that are difficult to read. The use of any script or italic font should be avoided. Stick to clear fonts that complement the concept and decor of your restaurant. Your printer literally has hundreds of different type styles for you to select from. Remember: Don't mix more than three different styles; they will make your menu look cluttered and distract the reader.

DAVE PAVESIC is a former restaurateur who now teaches hospitality administration at the university level. He previously owned and operated two casual-theme Italian restaurants in Orlando, Fla.; served as general manager of operations of a six-unit regional chain in the Midwest, operating four coffee shops, a fine-dining seafood restaurant and one drive-in; and was a college foodservice director. He currently teaches courses on restaurant cost control, financial management, and food production in the Cecil B. Day School of Hospitality Administration at Georgia State University in Atlanta, Ga. He has written numerous articles on menu-sales analysis, labor cost, menu pricing and equipment layout. His two other books are *The Fundamental Principles of Restaurant Cost Control*, Prentice Hall Publishers, 1998, ISBN 0-13-747999-9 and *Menu Pricing and Strategy*, fourth edition, Van Nostrand Reinhold Publishers, 1996, ISBN 0-471-28747-4.